MEXICO ACTIVITY BOOK

Author	Mary Jo Keller
Editor	Kathy Rogers
Page Design	Linda Milliken
Cover Design	Mary Jo Keller
Illustrations	Barb Lorseyedi
Consultant	Francisco Tapia

METRIC CONVERSION CHART

Refer to this chart when metric conversions are not found within the activity.

¼ tsp	=	1.25 ml	350° F	=	175° C
½ tsp	=	2.5 ml	375° F	=	190° C
1 tsp	=	5 ml	400° F	=	200° C
1 Tbsp	=	15 ml	425° F	=	220° C
¼ cup	=	60 ml	1 inch	=	2.54 cm
⅓ cup	=	75 ml	1 foot	=	30 cm
½ cup	=	120 ml	1 yard	=	91 cm
1 cup	=	240 ml	1 mile	=	1.6 km
			1 oz.	=	28 g
			1 lb.	=	.45 kg

EP073 • ©1996, 2003 Edupress, Inc.™ • P.O. Box 883 • Dana Point, CA 92629
www.edupressinc.com
ISBN 1-56472-073-X
Printed in USA

❖❖❖❖❖❖❖❖ TABLE OF CONTENTS ❖❖❖❖❖❖❖❖

adobe—a mixture of clay and mud which is formed into bricks and allowed to dry. The finished bricks are used for building houses.

Aztecs—a great civilization that established its empire near the modern day site of Mexico City. Their empire covered most of southern Mexico.

charreada—a rodeo, including competitions in roping, horsemanship, and steer wrestling.

charro—a Mexican cowboy or ranch hand.

charro suit—the national costume of Mexican men. It consists of a short jacket called a bolero and riding pants. It is often blue, trimmed with gold or silver buttons, and is worn with a sombrero.

jarabe tapatío—Mexican Hat Dance, a lively traditional dance performed all over Mexico.

macahuitl—a wooden sword used by Aztec warriors. It was edged with sharp pieces of volcanic glass.

mariachi—bands made up of six to eight strolling musicians, singing and playing horns, guitars, and a bass.

masa—corn kernels that have been cooked, soaked in lime water, and then ground. It is used to make tortillas, a Mexican flatbread.

Maya—civilization that developed in southern Mexico and in parts of Central America. They devised the most accurate calendar used up to modern times.

mestizos—descendants of Spanish settlers who married native Indians when they came to Mexico.

occidental—western.

Olmec—the first major civilization to develop in Mexico. They lived on the southern edge of the Gulf of Mexico.

oriental—eastern.

papel picado—a traditional art form of Mexico, created by cutting paper in decorative designs.

pelota—a Mexican ball game in which a hard rubber ball is bounced against a high wall by players wearing special baskets on their hands. It is known as the fastest game in the world.

pictographs—system of writing that was used by the Aztecs. Instead of letters, words were represented by pictures.

piñata—a hollow container made of clay or of papier mache. It is shaped as an animal or another object, and is covered with bits of colorful tissue and filled with candy and treats.

scribes—priests who were trained as writers. Scribes created the books left by the Aztec Empire.

sombrero—wide-brimmed Mexican hat made of felt or straw.

telpochcalli—boarding school where Aztec boys were sent to be trained as warriors.

tlachtli—a game similar to basketball that has been played by people in Mexico since ancient times.

Zapotecs—native civilization that developed in Southern Mexico. They were fierce warriors, and developed the first writing system in the Americas.

GEOGRAPHY

HISTORICAL AID

Mexico is the northernmost country of Latin America. It lies just south of the United States, the Rio Grande forming part of the border between the two countries. To the south Mexico borders the countries of Belize and Guatamala. The Pacific Ocean forms Mexico's western border and the Gulf of Mexico forms its eastern border.

Most of Mexico is mountainous. Two great mountain ranges extend along the coasts. They are called the Sierra Madre Occidental in the west and the Sierra Madre Oriental in the east. To the south lies a mass of mountains that includes a chain of volcanoes.

PROJECT

Learn about the geography of Mexico by coloring a map.

DIRECTIONS

1. Using the map of Mexico as a guide, follow the coloring directions on the next page.

MATERIALS

- One copy of map per student
- One copy of coloring directions per student
- Colored pencils (not crayons)
- Black pen
- Map of Mexico showing geographical features

1. Color the river between Mexico and the United States blue. Label it *Rio Bravo Del Norte,* its Mexican name.

2. Color the mountain range on the western coast brown and label it *Sierra Madre Occidental.* Color the mountain range on the east orange and label it *Sierra Madre Oriental.* What do you think the words *oriental* and *occidental* mean?

3. Color the area between the mountains green and label it the **Plateau of Mexico.** This area is home to most of the Mexican people and is the chief agricultural region. Add some corn stalks.

4. Mexico's three highest peaks, **Orizaba, Popocatepetl and Ixtacihuatl,** are volcanoes. **Paricutin** is another volcano. Connect these volcanoes with a thick red line. This is the **Volcanic Axis,** a series of volcanoes that extend across Mexico. Many of these volcanoes are active! Draw some smoke coming out of the volcanoes.

5. Color the area along the **Gulf of Mexico** purple. The northern part of this region is dry and covered with low thorny bushes and trees. Draw a thorny bush. The southern part is a tropical rain forest. Draw a big green tree.

6. Color the **Sierra Madre del Sur** yellow. The Aztecs found much of their gold in this area. Draw a gold nugget. What do you think the word *sur* means?

7. Color the **Yucatan Peninsula** pink. This area is a low limestone plateau. Great pits formed in the limestone by the rain were the sacred wells of the Maya. Draw a well.

8. Label the capital, **Mexico City.** Mark it with a big star.

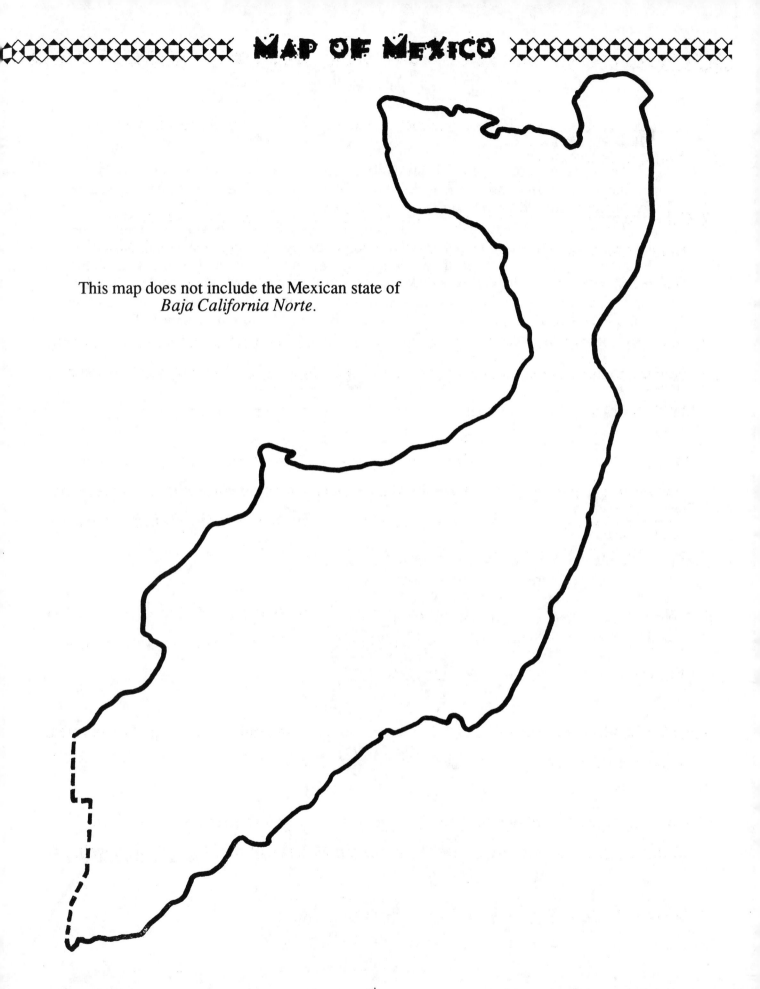

This map does not include the Mexican state of *Baja California Norte*.

FLAG

HISTORICAL AID

The Mexican coat of arms is an eagle perched on a cactus devouring a snake. A version of this coat of arms is featured on the Mexican flag. The green of the flag stands for independence, the white for religion and the red for union.

There is an interesting legend behind the coat of arms. A sun god named the *Hummingbird Wizard* or *Huitzitopochtli* told the ancient Aztecs to leave their home. He told the people to stop when they saw an eagle eating a snake and sitting on a cactus bearing red, heart-shaped fruit. The Aztecs wandered for 150 years looking for the sign. They found the place in which their god had told them to settle on an island in Lake Texcoco. They built the magnificent city of *Tenochtitlan* (Tay-nawch-TEE-tlan) which is now the area of Mexico City.

PROJECT

Make Mexican flags to decorate the classroom.

MATERIALS

- One copy of pattern per student
- Scissors
- Tape
- Crayons or colored pencils
- Red and green construction paper

DIRECTIONS

1. Color the coat of arms.

2. To assemble the flag, cut a piece of red and a piece of green construction paper the same size as the pattern page. Tape the colored paper to the pattern page with the green on the left and the red on the right.

EARLY MEXICO

The Indians of Middle America were the first farmers of the
New World. As early as 7000 B.C. farmers began cultivating
corn, beans, avocados, tomatoes, peppers and squash. They
raised turkeys for food. Without the need to constantly hunt for
food, the people had time for arts, crafts, trade and building. The
Maya and Aztec became two of the most advanced civilizations
in the Americas.

The Olmec—1200 to 200 B.C.
The first major civilization was the Olmec which developed along the southern edge of the Gulf of
Mexico. The Olmec people built cities, established trade with other native groups, developed a calendar
and a counting system. Sculptors carved massive stone heads as large as 9 feet (2.7 meters) tall and
weighing as much as 40 tons (36 metric tons)! They may have worshiped a god that was part human and

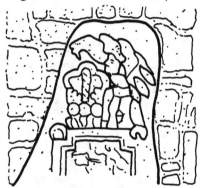

part jaguar. Jade figures and examples of beautiful pottery
have been found in the ruins of an Olmec pyramid and
ceremonial center at La Venta.

The Zapotecs—650 B.C. to 800 A.D.
The Zapotecs of southern Mexico were fierce warriors and
builders of great pyramids.
To build their religious center
at Monte Alban, Zapotec
engineers and builders
flattened an entire mountain
top and pulled all the materials for the pyramids and temples up the
sheer mountain wall! This advanced culture studied the stars and
developed the first writing system in the Americas, using hieroglyphics
(word-pictures) to record their history on stone tablets.

The Maya—350 B.C. to 900 A.D.
The Maya people built a magnificent civilization in southern Mexico
and parts of Central America. These native Americans produced
remarkable architecture, sculpture, painting and pottery. They devised a calendar more accurate than
any used up to modern times. Maya priests were both mathematicians
and brilliant astronomers who were able to plot the course of the planet
Venus with amazing accuracy.

The Aztec—1250 to 1520 A.D.
According to legend the Aztec were instructed by their god to settle on
an island in Lake Texcoco. By the 1400s the mighty Aztec armies had
built an empire that covered much of southern Mexico. There they
built the magnificent island city of Tenochtitlan, home to 100,000
people! Its major streets were canals spanned by drawbridges. At the
center of the city rose massive pyramids topped with temples where
thousands of human sacrifices were made.

OJO DE DIOS

HISTORICAL AID

Huichol Indians of present-day Mexico have kept many of their old traditions. Their dress, daily life and religious ceremonies reflect a culture rich in folk art with a deep respect for nature.

The *Ojo de Dios*, or God's Eye, is a well-known religious symbol of the Huichol. They believe that the design of the eye has power to heal and protect. The *Ojo de Dios*, or *Tsikuri*, is hung on the wall to be used in ceremonies and during prayer.

PROJECT

Make an *Ojo de Dios* by wrapping colorful yarn around crossed sticks.

MATERIALS

- Yarn in several bright colors
- Two sticks—these can be twigs, craft sticks, dowels or chopsticks
- Scissors
- Cardboard

DIRECTIONS

1. Make a cross with the two sticks by tying them together at the point where they cross with a strand of yarn.

2. Form a diamond shape by weaving the yarn from stick to stick, making a complete loop around each stick.

3. Add different color yarns as you go to create a bright pattern. When you have reached the ends of the sticks, glue the end of the yarn to the end of the last stick.

4. Make tassels to hang from each point by wrapping yarn around a piece of cardboard. On one side, thread another piece of yarn underneath and tie the ends. Use scissors to cut the yarn on the opposite side.

AZTEC WRITING

HISTORICAL AID

The Aztec people had no alphabet so they used *pictographs*, or little pictures, to represent words. For example, a picture of a foot meant "travel." Books were written by priests who were trained as *scribes*. The scribes primarily kept record books, but they also wrote books on history, religion, day-to-day living and even poetry!

Aztec books were written on pieces of tree bark that had been varnished and stuck together to make long strips, some as long as 35 feet (11 meters)! The scribe would draw on both sides of the paper, making sure that he drew the important people larger than the others. The book was then folded like an accordion.

PROJECT

Work as a cooperative group to make an Aztec manuscript using paper instead of wild fig tree bark.

MATERIALS

- White paper
- Pencils
- Scissors
- Crayons
- Tape

DIRECTIONS

1. Each student needs a sheet of white paper. Turn the paper sideways with the long side on top.

2. Use a pencil to sketch in the general outline of the story. Remember to make the more important figures larger than the rest! Use a vertical line to end a sentence or thought. Draw one story on each side, then color.

3. Lay out everyone's papers on the floor, end to end. Tape together to make a long manuscript. Fold the book accordion-style when you are finished.

AZTEC HEADDRESS

HISTORICAL AID

Aztec boys were trained to be warriors in a boarding school called a *telpochcalli*. They learned to use the *macahuitl*, a wooden sword edged with sharp pieces of volcanic glass. Warriors wore padded tunics and carried shields.

When a young warrior had taken three prisoners alive in battle, he was entitled to tie his hair up in a top knot and wear a feathered headdress.

PROJECT

Make an Aztec feathered headdress.

DIRECTIONS

1. Cut a crown shape from tagboard to fit around the head.

2. Glue on an assortment of decorations including disks cut from foil, bits of feathers, etc.

3. Staple or glue on the feathers as shown.

MATERIALS

- Tagboard
- Scissors
- Stapler
- Paintbrushes
- Sequins, glitter, foil paper, etc.
- Crayons or marking pens
- Feathers or feather shapes cut from construction paper

QUETZALCOATL

HISTORICAL AID

According to ancient legend, the god *Quetzalcóatl* once lived among the people of ancient Mexico and taught them medicine and farming. This gentle god told the people that human sacrifice was evil and that he preferred gifts of butterflies. *Quetzalcóatl* was driven out of Mexico by a rival god, but before he rode away on a winged serpent he promised to return and rule Mexico.

This god is represented as a feathered serpent and was associated with the planet Venus. Considered to be a great benefactor of mankind, *Quetzalcóatl* was the god of wisdom and knowledge.

PROJECT

Color a picture of the Indian god *Quetzalcóatl*.

MATERIALS

- One copy of pattern per student
- Scissors
- Crayons or markers

DIRECTIONS

1. Color the picture of *Quetzalcóatl* in the style of ancient Maya artists. Outline the figure in black, then color it in with solid colors. Maya artists rarely shaded the colors.

 CALENDAR

HISTORICAL AID

Maya priests used their highly advanced studies of astronomy and mathematics to develop two kinds of calendars. One was an almanac of 260 days. The days were named for different gods and goddesses. Priests used these calendars to predict good or bad luck.

The second type of calendar developed by the Maya had 365 days like our modern calendar. Instead of twelve months the Maya calendar had 18 months of 20 days each, with five days remaining at the end of the year. The Maya thought that these five days were extremely unlucky!

PROJECT

Make and use a calendar that demonstrates how the Maya calendar was used to name days.

MATERIALS

- Patterns for calendar on following page
- Scissors
- Colored pencils or crayons
- Tagboard or cereal boxes
- Brads
- Toothpicks
- Tape

DIRECTIONS

1. Color and cut out the calendar circles. Glue to tagboard and cut out. Tape toothpicks to the back of larger circle as shown.

2. Cut a rectangle of tagboard and use the brads to attach the circles to the tagboard so the circles barely touch.

3. Practice using the calendar.

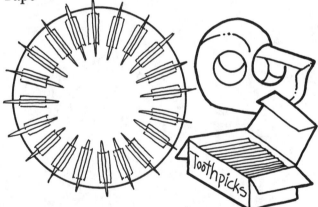

HOW TO USE THE CALENDAR

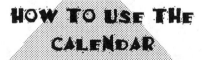

Notice how the wheels turn so that each day fits into a number. If you were to begin on 1 Rabbit, you would turn the wheels toward each other so that the next day would be 2 Water. When you get back to the number 1 again, you are starting a new cycle.

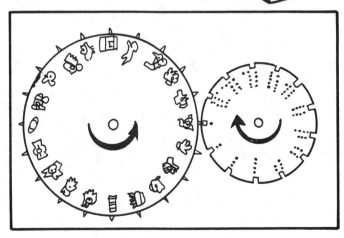

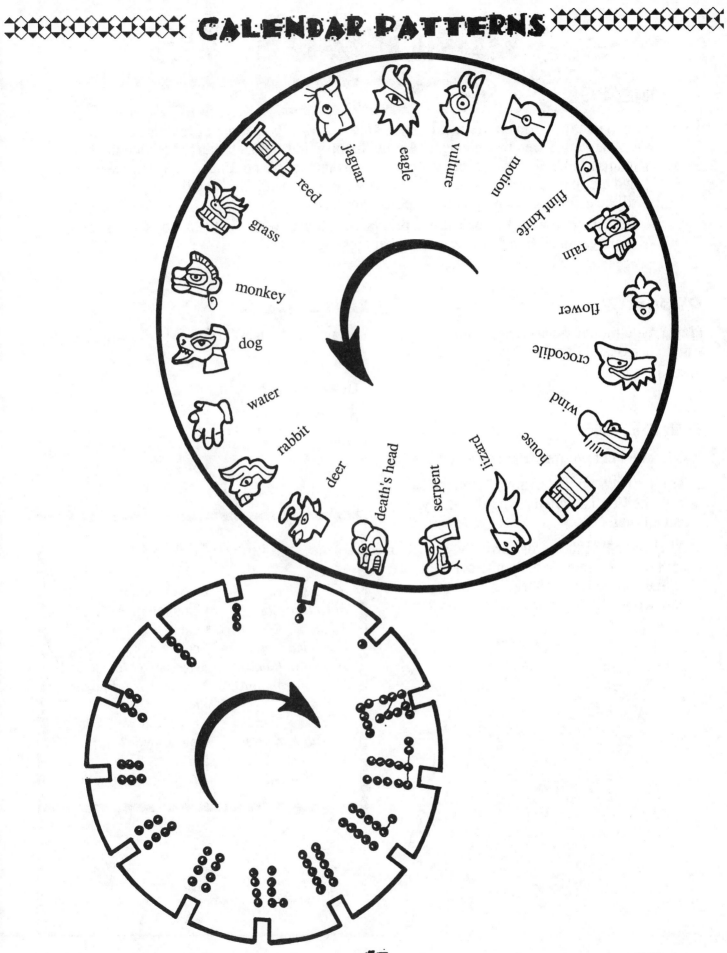

LANGUAGE

HISTORICAL AID

When the Spanish first came to Mexico in 1517, the people of middle America spoke many different languages. As the Spanish and Indian cultures blended the Spanish language spread, but in certain areas the people continued to speak their own language and the ancient languages were preserved. In Mexico today one can still hear the ancient Maya and Zapotec languages.

Today almost all Mexican people speak Spanish, which is the country's official language, in addition to their own tribal language.

PROJECT

Play a matching game and learn some simple phrases in Spanish.

DIRECTIONS

1. Color and cut out the language cards.

2. Try to match up the Spanish language card with the English language card that says the same thing.

3. After matching the cards correctly, glue them next to each other on the construction paper to make a reference sheet. Practice saying the new words you have learned with a friend.

MATERIALS

• Language Match Up Game (following page)

• Crayons

• Construction paper

• Scissors

• Glue

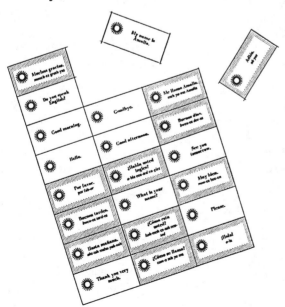

ANSWER KEY

¡Hola!	Hello.
Buenos días.	Good morning.
Buenas tardes.	Good afternoon.
Adiós.	Goodbye.
Hasta mañana.	See you tomorrow.
¿Cómo se llama?	What is your name?
Me llamo Amalia.	My name is Amalia.
Por favor.	Please
Muchas gracias.	Thank you very much.
¿Cómo está usted?	How are you?
Muy bien.	I'm fine.
¿Habla usted inglés?	Do you speak English?

Muchas gracias. *mooch*-as *grath*-yas	**How are you?**	**Adiós.** ad-*yos*
Do you speak English?	**My name is Amalia.**	**I'm fine.**
Good morning.	**Goodbye.**	**Me llamo Amalia.** meh *ya*-mo Amalia
Hello.	**Good afternoon.**	**Buenos días.** *bwen*-os *dee*-as
Por favor. por fab-*or*	**¿Habla usted inglés?** *a*-bla oos-*ted* en-*gles*	**See you tomorrow.**
Buenas tardes. *bwen*-as *tard*-es	**What is your name?**	**Muy bien.** *moo*-ee bee-e*n*
Hasta mañana. *ahs*-tah mahn-*yah*-nah	**¿Cómo está usted?** *koh*-moh es-*tah* oos-*ted*	**Please.**
Thank you very much.	**¿Cómo se llama?** *com*-o seh *ya*-ma	**¡Hola!** *o*-la

CLOTHING

HISTORICAL AID

The design of the clothing worn by people living in the villages dates back hundreds of years. In southern and central Mexico the men wear plain cotton shirts and trousers with sandals called *huaraches*. Women wear blouses and long, full skirts. They cover their heads with fringed shawls called *rebozos*.

PROJECT

Make traditional pieces of Mexican clothing.

MATERIALS

- Materials listed with each of the clothing projects on this and the following page

DIRECTIONS

1. Plan a day to make costumes. Arrange for a parent to sew the girls' skirts after they have "embroidered" them.

2. Wear the costumes at your class fiesta or hold a *paseo*. The *paseo* is an old Mexican custom. While chatting and listening to music in the evening, the girls walk in a clockwise direction around the plaza while the boys walk counterclockwise. If a boy wants to get a know a girl better, he will ask her to walk with him.

MAYA DRESS

The Maya woman of Yucatan wear long loose white dresses that are embroidered around the neck and bottom hem.

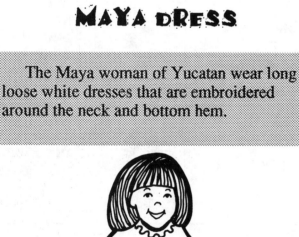

Center activity: Make a dress in the Maya style

Materials

- White t-shirt
- White sheet or fabric
- Scissors
- Crayons
- ½-inch (1.27 cm) wide elastic

Directions

1. Cut a piece of fabric to make a fairly long skirt and wide enough to go around the waist twice.

2. Color a design around the bottom of the fabric and around the neckline of the shirt. Press hard on the crayons to get a bright color.

3. Sew the skirt closed. Fold over the top of the fabric about ¾ inch (1.9 cm) and sew. Cut a piece of elastic to fit the waist. Insert into casing and secure with a few stitches.

SOMBRERO

A *sombrero* is a wide brimmed hat made of felt or straw that is worn as protection from the hot sun. The men's national costume — a dark blue *charro* suit with its short bolero jacket and riding pants with gold or silver buttons down the side, flowing red bow tie and spurred boots— is topped with a fancy white sombrero.

PONCHO

During the cold or rainy weather a man might wear the traditional *poncho*, which is a blanket that has a slit in the center for the head to go through. An unusual outer garment is worn in the Oaxaca state—a large cape made of straw!

Center activity: Make a poncho

Materials

• White sheet or muslin, cut in a 4 x 4-foot (1.2 m) square

• Crayons • Scissors

Directions

1. Color bold designs onto the muslin square including different color stripes.

2. Cut a slit in the center for your head to go through.

Center activity: Make a sombrero

Materials

• Heavy duty paper bowl

• Tagboard • Glue

• Scissors • Pencil

• Tempera paint • Paint brushes

• Yarn or string

Directions

1. Cut a large circle from tagboard—about 2 feet (61 cm) across. Cut a hole in the center of the tagboard that is slightly smaller than the diameter of the paper bowl. This is your cutting line.

2. Cut out the circle, and glue the bowl to the large circle as shown. Paint your sombrero to look like straw or felt.

3. Poke two holes in the brim. Cut a long piece of yarn or string. Thread it through the holes so the hat can be tied under the chin.

To complete this traditional costume:
• wear white pants or jeans and a white dress shirt
• wear sandals

FOLK ARTS

HISTORICAL AID

The work created by artists who have had no formal art training is called *folk arts*. These beautiful carvings, needlework, decorative items, and paintings are rarely signed by the artist and can be found at marketplaces throughout the world.

Modern Mexican folk art is rich in tradition. Examples of the beauty and variety of Mexican crafts can be found in the delicate feathered mosaics and tiny masks of jade, rock crystal, and turquoise carved by the early Indians, the wrought iron and gold work of the Colonial period, and the beautifully decorated pottery and textiles that Mexico is famous for throughout the world today.

PROJECT

Plan a day to make three Mexican folk arts.

MATERIALS

• See individual crafts on this and the following page

DIRECTIONS

1. Set up three centers in the classroom. Stock each with the materials for one of the three crafts described. Ask parent volunteers to help at each center.

2. Divide into three groups. Make a rotational schedule so that each group has time at all three centers. Allow time at the end of the day to share what was learned.

Brightly colored yarn is used in a variety of ways by Mexican folk artists. They create beautiful "paintings" by filling in the outline of their design with colorful yarns. Yarn is also used to add decoration to items such as this mirror.

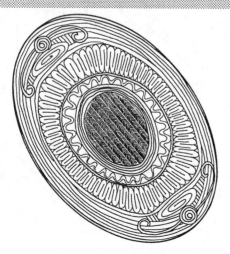

MIRROR

Center activity: Make a Mexican mirror plate

Materials

• Cardboard
• Aluminum foil
• Glue
• Scissors
• Yarn, assorted thicknesses and colors

Directions

1. Cut cardboard into an oval. Glue a large piece of aluminum foil into the center of the foil.

2. Cover the cardboard with yarn, leaving an oval shaped section of foil exposed in the center. Spread the glue in a thin layer, then press the yarn in place.

BARK PAINTING

Bark painting is a Mexican folk art that has its roots in ancient times. Early Middle American Indians stripped the bark from amate or wild fig trees to use as paper. Their paint was a mixture of powdered minerals mixed with plant juice!

Center activity: Make a bark painting

Materials
- Brown paper bags
- Tempera paints • Pencils
- Scissors • Paint brushes

Directions
1. Cut the paper bag to size.
2. Draw a design such as bird, tree, or flower, the most common themes of modern bark painting.
3. Paint in the design, leaving the background unpainted to show the "bark."

TIN LANTERN

Mexican folk artists use tin to make crowns to wear in processions, mirror frames, and other decorative items such as candle holders. These festive candle holders may be set on a table or hung from the ceiling. When many candle holders are hung from the ceiling at different heights the candlelight shining out from the holes makes beautiful flickering patterns on the walls and ceilings.

Center activity: Make a Mexican tin lantern

Materials
- Clean, empty tin cans
- Pencil • Paper • Tape
- Hammer • Big nails
- Newspaper
- Scissors

Directions
1. Cut the paper to fit the can. Draw a pattern of dots onto the paper and tape paper to the can.
2. Tightly roll folded newspaper and put inside the can. Use the hammer and nail to punch the holes.

 # MURALS

HISTORICAL AID

Mural painting is a Mexican art form that dates back to ancient times. Maya murals were painted on temple walls as early as 700 A.D. During the Spanish Colonial period artists painted beautiful murals in the churches.

In the 1900s artists such as Diego Rivera, David Alfaro Siqueiros and Jose Clemente Orozco created powerful murals that were vivid in color and bold in design. Their work appears in many public buildings, including some in the United States. These famous mural artists painted scenes from Mexican history. Many of the murals tell stories about the revolutions of the peasants and workers.

PROJECT

Paint a classroom mural in the style of the famous Mexican mural painters.

DIRECTIONS

1. Cover a wall with butcher paper.

2. Draw a design with pencil, covering as much of the area as possible. Choose an event that actually happened in Mexico or in your community as your mural's subject.

   OR: Project a scene onto the wall with the slide projector and trace the image with pencils.

3. Paint the design with brightly colored tempera paints.

MATERIALS

- White butcher paper
- Pencils
- Tape
- Tempera paint
- Paint brushes

Optional—slide projector

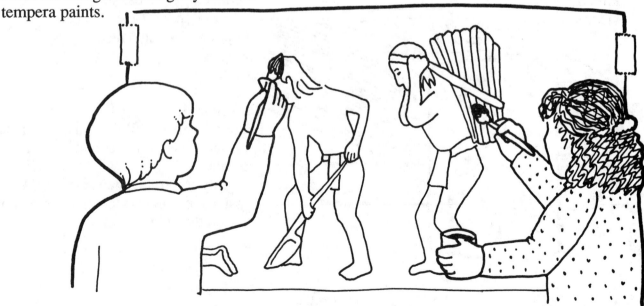

LACQUER WARE

HISTORICAL AID

Lacquer work in Mexico dates back to pre-Columbian times. Artisans of this period applied lacquer, a type of varnish, to the surface of wooden utensils for two reasons. Not only did the lacquer seal the wood and make it impervious to high temperatures and moisture, but it gave their work a rich, decorative sheen.

The two basic types of lacquer work found in Mexico today are an etched variety and a painted type that is used to decorate trays, bowls and dishes.

PROJECT

Make a bowl and plate that resemble Mexican lacquer ware.

DIRECTIONS

1. Paint both sides of the plate with dark blue, green or black paint. Let dry.

2. Paint a red stripe around the edge of the plate. Let dry.

3. Use the pencil to draw a design such as a bird, tree or flower onto the plate. Paint the design with bright, strong colors. Let dry.

4. When completely dry, spray plate with a spray-on sealer such as Krylon™, which is a kind of lacquer, to give the plate the sheen of lacquer ware.

MATERIALS

• Heavy duty paper plates
• Tempera paint
• Pencil
• Paintbrushes
• Spray-on sealer

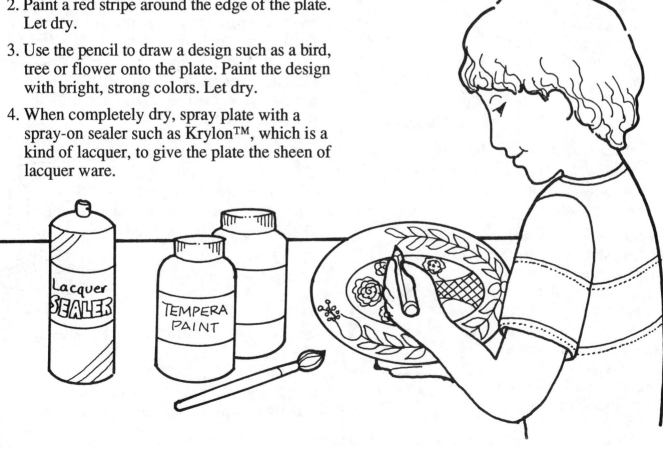

MEXICAN FOOD

HISTORICAL AID

The diet of modern Mexican people is very similar to that of the ancient Middle American Indians. The basis of most Mexican dishes is *maíz* (corn), beans and chili peppers. Popular foods eaten in Mexico today such as *tortillas, tamales,* and *pozole* (corn chowder) date from the time of the Aztecs. *Masa* is made from a large white corn kernel called *nixtamal* and is used to make corn tortillas. The dry corn is cooked and soaked in lime water for several hours, then ground while it is still wet, giving the *masa* its unique taste and texture.

Not all Mexican food is fiery hot, but most meals do come with a side dish of salsa and chili peppers. Diners can make their food as spicy as they like!

PROJECT

Prepare Mexican dishes to taste, or as part of a fiesta (page 36).

MATERIALS

• See individual recipes for ingredients and materials to prepare each dish.

Guacamole is made from mashed avocados which are native to Central America. Serve guacamole with tostada (tortilla chips) or as a sauce.

Mash 2 very ripe avocados until smooth. Add 2 teaspoons (10 ml) chili powder and lemon juice to taste.

Rice is another staple in the Mexican diet.

Cook 1 chopped onion in 1 tablespoon (15 ml) oil in electric skillet. Add 1 cup (250 ml) uncooked rice and cook, stirring constantly, for a few minutes until rice begins to color. Add 2⅓ cups (580 ml) beef broth, 1 cup (250 ml) canned tomato puree. Cover and cook about 25 minutes until rice is tender.

*Tacos are a form of Mexican sandwich. They are **tortillas** that are filled with a variety of things then folded or rolled.*

Set out bowls of cooked chopped beef or chicken, shredded lettuce, jarred salsa, and shredded cheese. Heat oil in an electric skillet. *(Caution: keep hot oil well away from children.)* Briefly heat corn tortilla in oil. Stack on a plate. Let children fill their own taco, fold and eat!

*Beans, or **frijoles**, are as important in the Mexican diet as tortillas, and like them, are served throughout the day. Often the beans are mashed and served as **frijoles refritos** (refried beans).*

Cover 1 pound (450 g) of dried pink or pinto beans with 6 cups (1.43 l) of water. Simmer over low heat for 12 hours. Add 1½ teaspoons (7.5 ml) salt and 2 tablespoons (30 ml) bacon fat. Continue cooking until beans are tender.

Mexican soup is either liquid, aguada, or dry, sopa seca. A dry soup is like a casserole.

Pozole (Corn Chowder)
- ¾ cup (185 ml) chopped onion
- 1 small can chopped green chilies, drained
- 1 teaspoon (5 ml) chili powder
- 1 tablespoon (15 ml) oil
- 3 cups (750 ml) chicken broth
- 2 15½ ounce (434 g) cans white hominy, drained

Saute onion, chilies and chili powder in 1 tablespoon (15 ml) oil for 7 minutes. Add broth; simmer 30 minutes. Add hominy and cook another 30 minutes. **Note: Hominy is dried corn that has been soaked in lime water.**

Cacao *was cultivated by the Indians long before the arrival of the Spanish. The Aztecs considered chocolate to be a special beverage and used cocoa beans as a form of money. The Aztecs made their hot chocolate with water. Mexican cooks roast and grind the cocoa beans at home! A* **molinillo** *is used to whip the hot* **cacao** *until it foams.*

Combine
- 2 cups (500 ml) milk
- 6 tablespoons (90 ml) sugar
- 2 ounces (56 g) unsweetened chocolate, cut into small pieces

Heat all ingredients in a large saucepan over low heat. Stir with a wire whisk until chocolate is completely dissolved. Turn up heat and bring to a boil. Allow mixture to bubble to the top of the pan. Remove from heat immediately and beat with whisk. Repeat boiling and beating 3 times. Tilt pan and beat well with whisk one more time.

A nutritious drink enjoyed at the marketplace is called a **liquado.**

Combine banana slices, strawberry halves, and sliced pineapple in the blender. Add orange juice to cover and liquefy.

*Mexican Wedding Cookies (**Polvorones**) are crumbly cookies that are baked for many traditional parties.*

Preheat oven to 350° F (180° C). Combine:
- 2 cups (500 ml) flour
- ⅔ cup (160 ml) sifted powdered sugar
- 1 cup (250 ml) chopped pecans
- 1 dash salt
- 1 teaspoon (5 ml) vanilla
- 1¼ cups (310 ml) softened unsalted butter

Work all ingredients together into a large dough ball. Shape into small balls and place on greased cookie sheet. Flatten slightly with a spoon. Bake 30 minutes or until slightly browned. Dust with powdered sugar when cool. Makes about 30 cookies.

A favorite dessert is a custard pudding called **flan**. *It is made of eggs, sugar and milk with a caramelized sugar glaze.*

Prepare a package of egg custard or flan according to the directions.

GAMES

HISTORICAL AID

Many ancient religious centers throughout Mexico had a special playing court for the game *tlachtli*, a kind of basketball. Only nobles were allowed to play this dangerous game that was also a type of religious ceremony. The losing team was sometimes sacrificed after the game to keep the gods happy!

In the late 19th century the Spanish introduced a handball game played with long curved baskets called *cestas*. This game is still being played in Mexico today in much the same form. Bullfighting was also introduced to Mexico by the Spanish, and remains a popular spectator sport to this day.

PROJECT

Plan a day of games from Mexico's past and present.

MATERIALS

• See each game on this and the following page for the supply list.

ANCIENT GAMES

◎◎ PATOLLI

Patolli was a popular game in ancient Mexico. Played with colored pebbles as markers and beans for dice, this game was very much like Parcheesi.

• Parcheesi set

Play a game of Parcheesi. You may wish to copy the playing board onto brown craft paper, and play with colored pebbles.

◎◎ TLACHTLI

Tlachtli is a game similar to basketball. Players tried to hit a rubber ball through a stone ring high on a wall without using their hands!

• Hula Hoop™ • Basketball • Duct tape

Tape a hula hoop to a pole. Players try to hit the ball through the hoop using only their hips, elbows or knees.

PELOTA

Pelota is known as the fastest game in the world. Players wearing a glove with a long wicker basket attached slam a hard rubber ball against a high wall. The ball travels at speeds over 155 miles per hour!

• Tennis rackets • Tennis ball • High wall

Two players alternately hit the ball against the wall. The first to miss loses the point.

SOCCER

Soccer is Mexico's most popular sport. Mexican soccer players are among the best in the world.

• Soccer ball • Chalk • Field or playground

Divide players into two teams. Mark goal lines with chalk. Players try to kick the ball across their goal line. No hands allowed!

BULLFIGHTING

Before some bullfights, the bulls are allowed to run through the streets. People run in front of the bulls or try to fight them as if they were matadors (bullfighters) in the ring!

Play a game of tag with the bull being "it." The fun of this game is there can be more than one "it!" When a player is tagged, he becomes a bull.

MUSIC & SONG

HISTORICAL AID

Traditional music can be heard at fiestas throughout Mexico! Mariachi bands are strolling groups of six to eight musicians. The members wear sombreros and dress in uniforms trimmed with silver sequins. When French soldiers married Mexican ladies they hired small bands for entertainment. The bands became known as mariachis after the French word for marriage.

Norteña or *ranchera* music is sung by ranch hands. Three musicians play an accordion, a guitar and a piece of wood! The leader sings and raps on a four-foot-long piece of wood that is wired to his belt. The leader must show the emotion of the song—if it is sad, he will actually cry.

PROJECT

Explore Mexican traditional music with a variety of activities.

MATERIALS

• Recordings of mariachi music, country and western music or other folk music

• Pencils

DIRECTIONS

1. Follow the directions to hear, sing and play traditional Mexican music.

SING IT!

*The famous folk song **La Cucaracha** (The Cockroach) was sung during the Mexican Revolution. In some of the verses, the soldiers make fun of their leader, Pancho Villa.*

Everyone knows the tune to **La Cucaracha**— practice singing it in Spanish!

La Cucaracha, La Cucaracha,
Ya no puede caminar.
Por que le falta, por que le falta,
De una patita de atrás!

HEAR IT!

There is usually a singer-leader, two horn players, two guitarists and a bass player in a mariachi band.
Listen to a recording of mariachi music. Can you hear all the instruments?

Call out "Ay-ay-ay-ay" at the sad parts.

PLAY IT!

Norteña music is often compared to American country and western music.
Listen to a recording of country and western music or folk music.

Play along by tapping on your desks with pencils.

Make your face match the music!

© Edupress

DANCE

HISTORICAL AID

Mexico's folk dances are some of the most beautiful and varied dances in the world. Many dance troops today still perform the ancient Maya and Aztec dances. The colorful costumes of the Conchero dancers include headdresses that are plumed with feathers over two feet long! The dancers move in a slow, circular pattern. Tied to their wrists and ankles are bracelets with tiny jingling bells attached to them,

The *jarabe tapatío*, or Mexican hat dance, is a lively dance with hopping steps and heel-and-toe tapping. This popular folk dance is performed everywhere from village fiestas to the Palace of Fine Arts in Mexico City, where it is danced regularly by the Ballet Folklórico.

PROJECT

Dance the *jarabe tapatío*, or Mexican hat dance.

MATERIALS

• Music to the Mexican hat dance

DIRECTIONS

1. Plan time to dance the *jarabe tapatío*, or make it an activity at a classroom fiesta.

2. Move the desks to the edges of the room.

3. Hop from foot to foot while the music is playing, clapping twice in between bars. Have fun swinging your partner during the refrain!

WEAVING

HISTORICAL AID

Hand weaving is an ancient Indian art and Mexican weavers are still famous for their beautiful home-woven fabrics. Throughout Mexico men wear colorful *serapes,* which are blankets worn over one shoulder. Because the styles of weaving vary in different parts of Mexico, the colors and designs woven into a serape tell where in Mexico it was made.

Belt loom weaving is a traditional method of weaving that dates back hundreds of years and is still in use. One end of the belt loom is tied to the weaver's waist and the other to a tree or fence. Weavers create beautiful strips of fabric on these simple looms.

PROJECT

Learn a simple type of weaving to make a colorful belt.

MATERIALS

• Heavy yarn in two bright colors

• Scissors

• Pencil

DIRECTIONS

1. Cut a piece of yarn long enough to go around your waist plus 24 inches (61 cm). Use that piece of yarn to measure and cut ten to twenty pieces of each color yarn, depending on how wide you want your belt to be.

2. Tie the yarn strands on the pencil, leaving ends long enough to make a fringe (see illustration). Tie the fringe ends together and tie or tape to the back of a chair or doorknob.

3. Start with the piece of yarn on the left and weave it over and under until it comes out on the right side. Always start on the left and follow the over and under pattern. Keep the yarn even and straight, remembering not to pull too tightly.

4. When you are finished, knot the end and slide out the pencil.

MARKETPLACE

HISTORICAL AID

Almost every village, city and town in Mexico has a marketplace. Going to the market is a very popular activity, especially in the farm areas. People who wish to sell the items they have brought to the market can rent a stall if they wish or just spread their goods on the ground.

People bring items such as baskets, lace, produce, food, crafts and pottery to sell or trade. The atmosphere in the marketplace is festive and noisy as people chat and visit with friends, and buyers and sellers bargain for the best deals.

PROJECT

Turn your classroom into a marketplace!

MATERIALS

- Small items brought from home to trade
- Beach towels

DIRECTIONS

1. With their parents' permission, have students bring a beach towel and a few small items from home to trade.

2. Push the desks to the side of the classroom. Students spread their towels on the floor and arrange their items. Children can take turns browsing through the market and being a vendor. Items may be traded several times!

VILLAGE LIFE

HISTORICAL AID

Many Mexican farmers live in small villages. The village plaza is the center of the community, and it is there that the church, government buildings and a few shops are located.

The shape and style of the village housing varies according to the climate. In the dry central area of Mexico the houses are made of *adobe,* a mixture of mud and clay that is formed into bricks and dried in the sun. In areas of heavy rainfall houses have walls built of poles covered with lime and clay, which is more water-resistant than adobe.

PROJECT

Make a classroom diorama of a Mexican village.

DIRECTIONS

1. Choose an area for the diorama and cover with brown paper.

2. Make houses, church and shops. Cut out the pattern on the following page from white construction paper and glue to a milk carton. Have an adult cut the door and window along the lines. Glue the paper to the carton to look like adobe. Glue the pasta onto the roof. When the glue is dry, paint the roof red to look like the red roof tiles. Add a tagboard steeple to the church.

3. Arrange buildings in the village. Paint in roads and fields of crops. Crumpled pieces of green tissue paper make good cabbages for the field.

4. Add finishing touches to the village. Glue twigs to small rectangles of tagboard to make kitchen lean-tos for the houses. Pave the street in the plaza with cobblestones made from small pebbles glued closely together. Make dirt roads by the farms by spreading a thin layer of glue and sprinkling on sand.

5. Color the people and animals. Glue to tagboard and cut out. Arrange them in the village.

MATERIALS

• 8 oz. (236 ml) milk containers

• Penne pasta (long, thin tube pasta)

• Tempera paint and paint brush

• White construction paper

• Scissors

• Pattern on following page

• Brown butcher paper

• Glue

• Twigs, pebbles, sand

• Tagboard scraps

• Green tissue paper

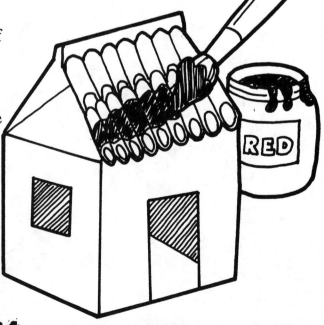

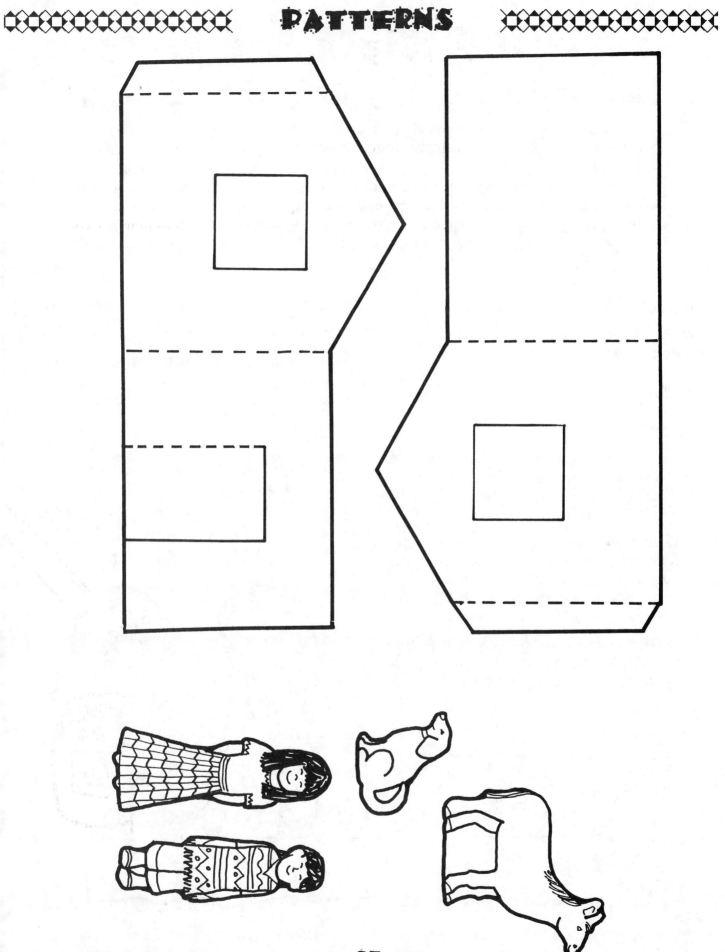

FIESTA

HISTORICAL AID

At a party you will always find good food and music! A party in Mexico is called a fiesta, and there are many fiestas throughout the year.

Each profession has a special day to celebrate its work. On the day honoring teachers, every student brings in a gift for the teacher. Even postmen have their own day on which each family on the postman's route offers him food and drink.

There are religious and patriotic festivals throughout the year as well. In addition, each town honors their patron saint or a special event in their history with an annual fiesta.

PROJECT

Work in cooperative groups to plan and carry out a Mexican fiesta.

DIRECTIONS

1. Divide into groups. Review the recipes and assign the responsibilities for each group. Arrange for parent help on fiesta day. Assign table setters and servers.

2. During the week before fiesta day make the decorations. Make a table covering by cutting butcher paper to fit the table tops and coloring with crayons or markers. Make costumes (pages 20-21) if desired.

3. On fiesta day, set up areas where each group will prepare its contribution to the feast. Turn on the music and enjoy your fiesta!

MATERIALS

- Recipes on pages 26-27
- Cooking utensils and ingredients for selected recipes
- Plastic utensils
- Paper bowls, plates and napkins
- Butcher paper
- Crayons or markers
- Decorations such as a *pinata* (page 46), or *papel picado* (page 41), or *cascarones* (page 38)
- Recording of Mexican *Mariachi* music

MASKS

HISTORICAL AID

Masks are frequently worn at fiestas, ceremonial celebrations, dance performances and theater productions in Mexico. The masks may be made from wood, papier-mache, cloth and gourds. Often the masks are made to symbolize different creatures from the animal world.

Mask making in Mexico has a long history. The ancient Maya carved small detailed masks from rock, crystal and marble. Mask makers of the Olmec tribe made masks in the image of their god who was part man and part jaguar. High ranking Aztec warriors wore wooden mask-like headdresses carved to look like eagles or jaguars.

PROJECT

Make a mask using a variety of craft materials.

DIRECTIONS

1. Set out the art materials, scissors and glue. Students can choose to build their mask on a paper plate, paper bag or tagboard shape.

2. Students can use their imaginations to decorate their mask. Staple yarn to any mask that needs to be tied on.

MATERIALS

- Heavy duty paper plates or platters
- Tagboard
- Paper bags
- Variety of art materials such as:
    colored construction paper
    foil
    sequins
    raffia
    foam meat trays
    egg carton sections
    chenille sticks
    pom-poms
    feathers
    rick-rack
- Scissors
- Glue
- Stapler
- Yarn or string

CINCO DE MAYO

HISTORICAL AID

The national holiday *Cinco de Mayo,* which means May 5th, honors the Battle of Puebla on that date in 1862. It was during this battle that untrained Mexican forces defeated an army of French mercenaries.

Cinco de Mayo is celebrated with boisterous fiestas throughout Mexico. In Mexico City, the president makes a stirring speech that is followed by a huge military parade through the streets of the capital.

Local celebrations include *mariachi* bands, ferris wheels, fireworks, dancing and lots of delicious food and drink!

PROJECT

Celebrate Cinco de Mayo with a classroom fiesta (page 36). Make *cascarones* to have at your fiesta. Make sure you have a broom nearby!

DIRECTIONS

1. Use a large sewing needle to pierce a raw egg on both ends. Cut a small hole in one end. Blow into the small hole over a bowl to catch the raw egg. Rinse the egg and allow to dry thoroughly.

2. Fill eggs with confetti. Seal the opening by gluing a small piece of tissue paper over the opening.

2. Paint the egg with bright colors.

MATERIALS

• Empty egg shells—see directions
• Tissue paper
• Scissors
• Glue
• Confetti
• Tempera paint
• Paint brushes

Cascarones or Mexican confetti eggs are very popular at fiestas. Boys and girls hope to crack an egg over the head of someone they secretly like. By the end of a fiesta a very popular boy or girl may be covered in confetti.

DÍA DE LA RAZA

HISTORICAL AID

Día de la Raza (Day of the Race), is a very important holiday in Mexico. On this day the Mexican people celebrate their mixture of people, races and cultures with pride. Columbus Day, October 12th, is the day chosen for this celebration, as *Cristóbal Colón* as he is called in Spanish, symbolizes the birth of the Mexican race.

It was Columbus who opened the way for the Spanish to come to middle America where they married the native Indians and created a new race called *mestizos*. Today, seven out of ten Mexicans are *mestizos*.

PROJECT

Celebrate the different ethnicity of the students in your class with a sharing day.

MATERIALS

• Items or photographs brought from home

DIRECTIONS

1. Assign each student to bring in a photograph or an item that tells something about his family's ethnic background. Have each student write a paragraph telling the history of the item he brought to show.
2. Give each student time to share his family's history during your class's *Día de la Raza*.

DÍA DE LOS MUERTOS

HISTORICAL AID

On October 31st people in Mexico begin a three day festival known as *El Día de los Muertos* (Day of the Dead). Small cups of hot chocolate, candles and sugar skulls are placed on an altar to invite the *angelitos*, or spirits of deceased children, to come back for a visit.

The following day is a day of visiting and feasting. The large altar is arranged with loaves of bread, flowers, fruit, and the favorite foods the relatives enjoyed in life. Candles are lit, and fireworks signal that the spirits are on their way home. For the next 24 hours the church bells will ring continuously.

November 2nd marks the last day of the celebration with a trip to the cemetery to bring flowers, enjoy a picnic and visit.

PROJECT

Bake *pan de muertos*, a special sweet bread made for *El Día de los Muertos*.

DIRECTIONS

1. Let dough rise following label directions until doubled in volume. Punch down and turn onto a lightly floured surface.

2. Cut off a small piece of dough for decoration. Shape the remaining dough into a round loaf. Roll the reserved dough into a long thin rope. Lay it on top of the bread in the shape of a flower, moistening it slightly if necessary.

3. Let the dough rise in a warm place until doubled in bulk, about 1 hour.

4. Bake at 350° F (180° C) for 30-35 minutes.

5. Make icing while bread is cooling. Mix 1 cup (250 ml) sifted confectioners' sugar and 1 teaspoon (5 ml) lemon juice with 3-4 teaspoons (15-20 ml) very hot water. Drizzle over bread in small loops. Sprinkle with multi-colored sugar.

MATERIALS

- 1 loaf frozen bread dough
- Flour
- Cookie sheet
- Oven mitts
- Knife
- Confectioners' sugar
- Sifter
- Lemon juice
- Colored sugar

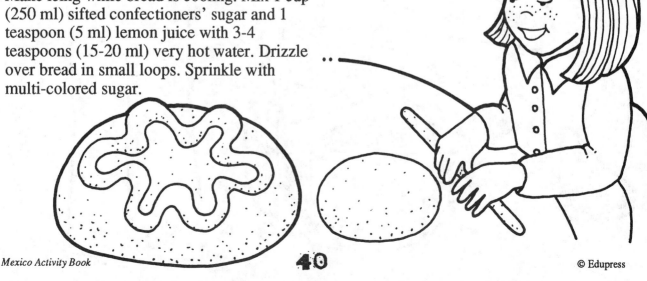

PAPEL PICADO

HISTORICAL AID

Papel picado, or paper cutting, is a traditional art in Mexico that dates back to pre-Columbian times. This delicate paper craft is usually created to decorate an area where a festival will take place. On *El Día de los Muertos* (Day of the Dead) families set up *ofrendas*, or banquet tables, to celebrate the one-day visit of deceased relatives. These tables are often decorated with strings of *papel picado*.

The designs of *papel picado* may be very simple or may be so intricate that a special paper chisel must be used to cut the design.

PROJECT

Decorate the classroom with *papel picado*.

MATERIALS

- Brightly colored tissue paper
- Scissors
- Glue stick
- String

DIRECTIONS

1. Fold tissue paper evenly. Cut out a design. or a scene.

2. Stretch string all around the classroom. Glue the papel picado to the string—fill the entire length!

LAS POSADAS

HISTORICAL AID

People have been celebrating *Las Posadas* since it was introduced to Mexico by Fray Diego de Soria in 1587. On the nine nights before Christmas, friends and neighbors gather to recreate the journey of Mary and Joseph to Bethlehem and their search for lodging on the night of Christ's birth. These ceremonies are called *posadas*, which means *inn* or *lodging*.

With lighted candles the procession goes from house to house where shelter is denied. Finally they come to a home where they are welcomed with refreshments and a piñata game for the children.

PROJECT

Participate in the custom of *Las Posadas* by traveling to other classrooms looking for shelter.

DIRECTIONS

1. Arrange with three other teachers to visit their classrooms. Plan for refreshments and a piñata to be at the last classroom. Make copies of the Las Posadas verses to distribute. Students are encouraged to dress in traditional costumes.

2. When the class arrives at the first "inn," have them knock on the door, then call out the first verse. The "innkeeper" and her class respond with the second verse. Repeat.

3. At the last classroom, enjoy refreshments and a piñata game.

MATERIALS

• *Las Posadas* verses on following page

• Traditional costumes, pages 20-21

• Hot chocolate, page 27 (or a mix)

• *Polvorones*, page 27

• Piñata

• Candy to fill the piñata

• Cups and napkins

SPANISH	ENGLISH
Peregrinos:	**Pilgrims:**
En nombre del cielo	In the name of heaven,
Os pido posada,	I ask you for lodging.
Pues no puede andar,	My beloved wife
Mi esposa amada.	Can no longer go on.
Posadero:	**Innkeeper:**
Aquí no es mesón	This is not a hotel.
Sigan adelante,	Go on ahead.
Yo no puedo abrir,	I can't open the door,
No sea algún tunante.	You may be bad people.
Peregrinos:	**Pilgrims:**
Posada te pide,	Lodging I ask of you,
Amado casero,	Friend innkeeper,
Por sólo una noche,	For just one night,
La Reina del Cielo.	For the Queen of Heaven.
Posadero:	**Innkeeper:**
Pues si es una reina,	Well, if she's a queen
Quien lo solicita,	Who asks for it,
¿Cómo es que de noche,	How come she travels
Anda tan solita?	Alone at night?
Peregrinos:	**Pilgrims:**
Mi esposa es María,	My wife is Mary,
Es Reina del Cielo,	She is Queen of Heaven,
Y madre va a ser,	And she is going to be the mother
De Divino Verbo.	Of the Holy Child.
Posadero:	**Innkeeper:**
¿Eres tú José?	Are you Joseph?
¿Tu esposa es María?	Is your wife Mary?
Entren peregrinos.	Come in pilgrims.
No los conocía.	I did not know who you were.
Entren santos peregrinos,	Come in holy travelers,
Reciban este rincón,	Take this corner in the stable.
Que aunque es pobre la morada,	Even though this place is poor,
Se la doy de corazón.	I give it to you with all of my heart.

GUADALUPE DAY

HISTORICAL AID

Guadalupe Day, December 12th, is Mexico's most important religious holiday. On this day people from all over Mexico journey to the chapel on Tepeyac Hill in Mexico City, where it is believed that the mother of Jesus appeared to an Indian peasant named Juan Diego.

The festival begins the night before with dance performances and parties, but throughout Guadalupe Day people come to the church to pray. Many of them pin *milagros (*which means *miracles)* to the wall near the statue of the Virgin of Guadalupe. These small silver or tin objects are shaped like hearts, arms or legs, and symbolize the giver's thanks for a cure.

PROJECT

Make paper roses and tin ornaments to celebrate Guadalupe Day.

MATERIALS

• See projects on next page

DIRECTIONS

1. Celebrate Guadalupe Day with a fiesta (page 36) that includes making paper flowers and *milagros.*

THE STORY OF THE VIRGIN OF GUADALUPE

Mexicans believe that in 1531 Mary, the mother of Jesus, appeared to an Indian named Juan Diego. She asked Juan to go to the bishop and request that a church be built on the hill so she could be close to her people. When the bishop asked for a sign that the woman was indeed the Blessed Virgin, Juan opened his cape to show the roses that had sprung up at the site where roses had never grown before. But the bishop did not look at the roses. He gazed instead at the picture of the woman who had appeared to Juan on the inside of his cape. No one could explain how it got there! Juan's cape, or *tilma,* still hangs in the church built there.

GUADALUPE DAY

PAPER ROSES

Materials

- Red tissue or crepe paper
- Green construction paper
- Chenille sticks
- Scissors
- Tape or glue

Directions

1. Cut crepe paper into 10-inch (25.4 cm) squares.

2. Lay 10-12 sheets on top of each other and accordion pleat. Wrap a chenille stick tightly around the middle and twist securely. Gently separate the tissue and fluff to make a rose.

3. Cut leaves from construction paper and tape or glue to the back of the flower.

MILAGROS

Materials

- Tagboard
- Aluminum foil
- Pencil • Scissors
- Toothpick • Tape
- Permanent markers (optional)

Directions

1. Cut a mitten or heart shape from the tagboard. Cover with aluminum foil.

2. Use a toothpick to gently inscribe details and your name on the *milagro*. Decorate with marker.

3. Tape to the wall of the classroom.

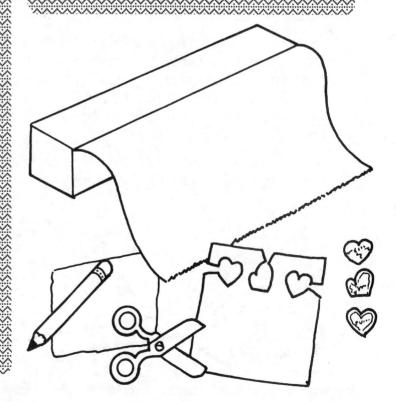

PIÑATA

HISTORICAL AID

    Piñatas are containers made of earthenware or papier mache. Many are shaped like animals, most commonly dogs or donkeys.

    The piñata is filled with candy, fruit and toys. It is hung above the heads of the children from the ceiling or a tree. The children are blindfolded, and each gets a turn to hit the piñata with a stick until it breaks and showers down the treats!

    Piñatas are a favorite treat at fiestas and are part of special celebrations at Easter and at Christmas.

PROJECT

Make a sun piñata and play the Piñata game.

DIRECTIONS

1. Inflate the balloon. Tear the newspaper or paper toweling into small pieces. Combine equal parts glue and water in a large disposable container.

2. Dip the paper pieces in the glue and cover the balloon with several layers of paper. Let dry.

3. Cut a hole in the top of the piñata and remove the balloon. Paint the piñata yellow. When the paint dries, add a smiling sun face. Make cones from the construction paper and hang streamers from the ends. Glue to the piñata to make the sun's rays.

4. Poke two holes at the top of the piñata. Attach the string to make a handle for hanging.

MATERIALS

- Large balloon
- Newspaper or paper towels
- 1 pint (473.6 ml) white glue
- Tempera paint
- Paint brush
- Yellow construction paper
- Colored streamers or tissue paper
- Sturdy string or twine
- Small candies
- Blindfold
- Broom

LOS REYES MAGOS

HISTORICAL AID

Children in Mexico do not usually receive their gifts on Christmas Day. On the evening of January 5th, children set out their shoes with a note to the Wise Men telling them what they want. According to religious belief, it was the Three Wise Men that brought gifts to the baby Jesus on this day about 2,000 years ago.

The next day families share a sweet bread called *rosca* made in the shape of a large doughnut. It contains a tiny porcelain doll made to represent the baby Jesus. The person that finds it must donate a statue to the church on February 2nd and host a reception!

PROJECT

Celebrate *Los Reyes Magos* by making and eating holiday cakes.

MATERIALS

- Cupcake mix
- Baking cups
- Aluminum foil

DIRECTIONS

1. Make cupcake batter as package directs. Twist a small piece of aluminum foil into the shape of an infant. Drop it into one of the cups of batter. Bake as directed.

2. Serve the cupcakes to the class. The person who finds the doll in his or her cupcake becomes its *padrino,* or godfather, and must bring in a treat for the class!

RODEO

HISTORICAL AID

The area around the Rio Grande Santiago in the Mexican state of Jalisco is known for its farms and ranches. It was here that the Mexican rodeo, or *charrida*, was created by the ranch hands in the 18th century. These early competitions included roping, horsemanship and steer wrestling. Mexican cowboys, called *charros*, later organized *charridas* in the United States where they became known as rodeos.

The words *lariat, lasso, stampede,* and *rodeo* are all words used in the United States that came from the Mexican *charros*.

PROJECT

Learn a knot tied by *charros* and practice aiming and throwing a rope at a target.

MATERIALS

- 15-foot (4.5 m) length piece of rope
- Target, such as a chair

DIRECTIONS

1. Follow the directions to tie a bowline in the rope to make a loop.

2. Loosely coil the rope in your left hand, keeping your hand cupped around the rope, not tightly closed. Hold the rope below the loop in your right hand.

2. Stand with your right shoulder facing the target. Swing the rope while you aim, then toss the rope and lasso your target.